KU-032-565

Contents

Jess to the rescue   4

   A visit with Grandma   4

   Grandma's problem   6

   A class trip   8

   Finding a solution   10

   A real success story   12

What's the issue?   14

Digging deep   16

Coal-powered future   18

Making energy around
the world   20

What's your opinion?   22

Think tank   24

Glossary   24

Index   25

Look for the **Thinking Cap**.
When you see this picture, you will find
a problem to think about and write about.

Jess to the rescue

A visit with Grandma

Jess lives in a small coal mining town in western Canada. Every Sunday, she rides her bike to visit her grandmother. Jess loves these Sunday visits. Grandma always has something interesting to discuss. They bake biscuits and have a long lunch together, chatting the whole time.

About half of Canada's coal is transported by train. Canada's coal trains can be more than a kilometre long! They can carry more than 16,000 tonnes (15,150 tons) of coal in as many as 125 wagons.

Written by Sarah Irvine
Illustrated by John Bennett

Canada

My name is Lucas. I live in Toronto, Canada. Our electricity comes from a coal-fired power station. The power station produces a lot of pollution – about the same as 3,500,000 cars! Now there are plans to close down the plant. What can people use instead of coal to make electricity?

This morning, Jess was running late, so she decided to take a short cut around the back of the coal mine. Just as Jess got to the railway crossing, the barrier came down.

'Oh no, now I'm going to be really late,' she muttered.

Jess watched the train approach and covered her nose and mouth with her sleeve. She didn't want to breathe in any of the coal dust. The train made a lot of noise and took ages to pass. Jess counted 112 wagons full of coal. Finally, the barrier lifted, and Jess dashed across the tracks.

Grandma's problem

Jess knocked on her grandmother's front door and poked her head in.

'Good morning, Grandma,' she called. Grandma looked up from her seat at the kitchen table and smiled.

'Good morning, dear. You're just the person I need to help me,' she said.

Jess looked at the table. It was covered with photos, leaflets and maps of the coal mine. Jess's grandmother was the community **spokesperson** for the mining company. Once a month, she met with the company to talk about mining issues that might affect the people or wildlife in the area.

'What's the problem, Grandma?' asked Jess.

Her grandmother sighed. 'The mine needs to build a very long conveyor belt. It will carry coal from the mine, across the river to the processing plant. However, it will stop deer and other wildlife from getting to the river to drink. If the company can't build the conveyor belt, the mine will close. Many people will lose their jobs.'

This was definitely a problem, Jess thought. Her parents both worked for the mine.

spokesperson person who speaks on behalf of others

Coal mining companies often employ many people from local areas to work at the mines. They also create other jobs in the area and employ local tradespeople.

A class trip

The next day, Jess talked to her teacher about her grandmother's problem. Mr Haley thought it would be a good idea for the whole class to talk about it. Many of Jess's classmates had family members who worked at the mine. It was a problem that affected them too.

One of Jess's classmates suggested they go on a class trip to see the area where the mining company planned to build the conveyor belt. After school, Jess got the maps and plans from her grandmother, and Mr Haley organised the trip.

A mine is a noisy place. Trucks, trains, conveyor belts and heavy machinery can disturb local people and wildlife.

The next morning, the whole class piled into the school bus. The bus driver followed the map and soon arrived at the site. As the bus stopped, Jess saw two elk run into the forest. When she stepped out of the bus, she noticed the ground was covered with different animal tracks leading down to the river. Her grandmother was right. This was a busy place for local wildlife!

Finding a solution

Back at school, the students wrote letters to the mining company with their suggestions. Each person had an opinion. Some students thought that the conveyor belt should not be built. Others thought that the wildlife would find somewhere else to drink. Some suggested different ways to build the conveyor belt. Jess gave all the letters to her grandmother to take to the meeting on Friday night.

Early Saturday morning, Jess rode over to Grandma's house. She was anxious to find out what had happened at the meeting.

When Jess arrived, her grandmother gave her a big hug.

'Guess what?' Grandma said. 'They used a suggestion from your class. They're going to build the conveyor belt three metres above the ground.

'Animals will be able to walk under the conveyor belt to use the river. The coal will still get to the processing plant, everyone will still have their jobs and the wildlife can still use the river.

'Thank you very much for your help, Jess. By working together, your class found a solution that will keep everyone happy!'

A real success story

Jess's story is fiction. However, it was inspired by a true story about a coal mine in British Columbia, Canada. A conveyor system was built with some sections about three metres (ten feet) above the ground to create underpasses for elk and other wildlife to reach the river. It was a great success! After the conveyor system was built, scientists continued to monitor wildlife in the area. Their studies showed that local wildlife adapted well.

In Canada, coal mining is an important industry that employs about 56,000 people. About half of Canada's coal is **exported**. It is used to generate electricity, and to make steel and cement.

export to send goods to another country for sale

Coal mining is an important industry in Canada. However, it can affect local communities and wildlife. Write down your thoughts about these questions so that you can talk about them with a classmate.

1. What were the problems that were mentioned in Jess's story? What are some other problems that might be caused by coal mining?

2. How could these problems be solved? How would you solve them?

What's the issue?

Electricity powers much of our daily lives. Think about all the things you use every day that need electricity. Then imagine what your life would be like without electricity.

We use energy to generate electricity. **Fossil fuels**, such as oil, natural gas and coal, are some of the most common sources of energy. But oil and natural gas are becoming more expensive. They are being used up quickly, and the available supplies are running out. Coal is cheaper than oil and natural gas, and there is more of it. Many countries around the world use coal to make electricity.

However, mining coal and using it to make electricity can affect the environment. It can also cause problems for local communities. Like oil and natural gas, coal is a natural resource that will one day run out. What will happen then?

fossil fuel fuel that has formed underground from plant or animal remains

Coal-fired electricity

Coal is used to generate nearly half the world's electricity. To make coal-fired electricity, coal is burned to heat water. This creates steam, which is used to spin turbines. The turbines turn generators, which create electric power.

Burning coal releases many harmful toxins into the air, such as:

- **Sulphur dioxide**
  This is a major cause of acid rain, which can kill trees, harm animals and damage buildings.

- **Carbon dioxide**
  Scientists believe that high levels of carbon dioxide may contribute to climate change.

- **Mercury**
  This metal builds up in fish, making them unsafe to eat.

How long will it last?

Some scientists estimate that if people continue to use natural resources at today's rate, this is how long they will last:

Oil	40–60 years
Natural gas	70–120 years
Coal	220–250 years
Water	Forever
Wind	Forever
Solar energy	Forever

Digging deep

Coal has formed over millions of years from the remains of plants. Coal is found on every continent. It is mined in several different ways. In the past, much of the coal in Canada came from underground mining. Deep shafts were dug down to reach coal that lies far below the surface. Then tunnels were dug from the shafts to reach the coal.

Today, most of Canada's coal comes from surface mining. This involves clearing away all the soil, rocks and trees from the land above the coal. The exposed coal is then dug up. Coal is transported away from mines by trains, by trucks or on conveyor belts.

Mining can cause major changes to a landscape and ecosystem. Many countries, including Canada, have laws to make sure mining companies protect local people and wildlife. There are often laws that require mining companies to leave an area as close to its original condition as possible.

Put on your thinking cap

Mining and transporting coal can cause many problems. Write down your thoughts about these questions so that you can talk about them with a classmate.

1. How could people prevent mines from destroying the habitats of plants and animals?

2. How could people prevent chemicals and dust from mines from polluting the air and water?

3. How might noise pollution from heavy mining machinery, trucks and trains be reduced?

This cutaway diagram shows coal being mined from an underground coal mine.

Coal-powered future

Several countries around the world, including India and South Korea, are joining the United States in its FutureGen project. The project involves the building of a new type of power station that will be the world's first environmentally friendly, coal-fuelled power station. It will use coal to produce hydrogen gas and electricity without producing harmful emissions. The project will cost about $1.5 billion and take 10 years to complete.

Instead of burning coal, the power station will use a process called **coal gasification** to make hydrogen gas and electricity.

coal gasification process that changes coal from a solid to hydrogen gas, so the gas can be burned to make electricity

> FutureGen might solve environmental problems caused by burning coal for electricity, but coal would still need to be mined. Do the environmental effects of mining outweigh the benefits of FutureGen?

Above: An artist's drawing of what the power station may look like

Project members want the hydrogen to be used instead of petrol in future cars, trucks and buses. Using hydrogen will help reduce pollution. It is hoped that many power stations like the FutureGen one will soon open around the world.

Coal mine workers

Traditional methods of coal mining also affect the health and safety of workers in coal mines. In the past, coal was mined by hand, and many workers died in mining accidents. Many more died of lung diseases from breathing the coal dust.

In industrialised countries today, machines do much of the digging, and workers wear safety gear. However, few jobs are more dangerous or more difficult than working in a coal mine.

These workers in China form a human conveyor belt as they transport coal to waiting barges.

Making energy around the world

Wind power

DENMARK – Wind turbines use the power of the wind to make electricity. Some wind farms are on land. Some, like this wind farm off the coast of Denmark, are in the ocean. The wind flows fairly constantly over water, because there is nothing blocking its path.

Sugar power

TANZANIA, AFRICA – When sugar cane has been crushed and the juice removed, the leftover material is called bagasse. In Tanzania, bagasse is burned to produce electricity to run the sugar mills. Any extra electricity is sold to the **national grid**.

national grid the country's electric power network

Solar power

CALIFORNIA, UNITED STATES – SunLine Transit Agency in Coachella Valley uses sunlight to produce clean, renewable electricity. The company then uses this to make hydrogen to run its fleet of environmentally friendly buses.

Wave power

SCOTLAND, UNITED KINGDOM – The world's first commercial wave power station has opened on the island of Islay. The motion of waves is used to make electricity. The station provides power to about 400 local households.

Dung power

DEVON, ENGLAND – The UK's first dung-fired power station is in operation. The station uses about 166,000 tonnes (163,500 tons) of **slurry** a year to produce methane gas. The gas then powers the station, producing electricity for the national grid. The process also produces organic manure for local farmers. There are about 40 dung power stations across Germany and Denmark.

slurry   mixture of water, mud and animal waste

What's your opinion?

Both mining and burning coal affect the environment.
Wind and rain transport the harmful chemicals in coal
smoke long distances. This means that coal burned in
one country can have harmful effects in other countries.

- Coal is one of the world's cheapest and most plentiful
  fossil fuels, but are the environmental costs of mining
  and burning coal too high? Explain your answer.

- Should countries around the world work together
  to keep the coal supply from running out too quickly?
  How could this cooperation be achieved?

- Should there be global rules about burning coal
  to reduce environmental problems around the world?
  Why or why not?

I don't think people should burn coal
unless they have a power station like
the FutureGen one. The plant will get rid
of a lot of the yucky stuff that goes
into the air from burning coal. Also,
it'll be great if we use hydrogen instead
of petrol in cars. This will make the air
better to breathe, and we'll be healthier.

Mum told me that she saw a TV show that suggested that waste ponds could collect the harmful chemical pollutants from mines. It also said that the noise at mines could be reduced with a special muffler on the trucks. So I don't think the situation is so bad.

When people dig for coal, they disturb animals and plants. I don't like that. People need to find a better way of making energy rather than using coal. I think using a renewable form of energy, such as water or wind, is a great idea.

Think tank

1 What do you think will happen when people have used up all the coal?

2 Do you think people should spend more time and money developing other alternative fuels? What could result from this?

Do your own research at the library, on the Internet, or with a parent or teacher to find out about how you can save energy and learn about what some people are doing to find alternative fuels.

Glossary

coal gasification process that changes coal from a solid to hydrogen gas, so the gas can be burned to make electricity

export to send goods to another country for sale

fossil fuel fuel that has formed underground from plant or animal remains

national grid country's electric power network

slurry mixture of water, mud and animal waste

spokesperson person who speaks on behalf of others